LINCOLN

the archaeology of an historic city
by Christina Colyer
Director of Excavations,
Lincoln Archaeological Trust

Photographs by H.N. Hawley and C. Colyer
Cover design, layout & drawings by Carol George
© 1975 Lincoln Archaeological Trust

This booklet is designed to describe to the increasing numbers of interested non-specialists some of the recent archaeological work in Lincoln, particularly the sites excavated since 1970 under the direction of the author. No apology is made for the uneven distribution of information between one period of Lincoln's past and another, nor between different aspects of the city's material development, for the available archaeological evidence is itself unevenly distributed. Inevitably some prominence has been given here to those periods and facets of Lincoln's history about which the least is known, where archaeological discoveries can contribute most to our knowledge.

This is an interim statement concerned with evidence which is itself frequently ambiguous, and accordingly the text is peppered with words or phrases expressing doubt. Further excavation is required to answer specific problems, and the interpretation of the information already obtained may be altered by further research and analysis. The picture changes as each new piece of evidence is taken into account and as accepted theories are questioned, answered and questioned again. Much of the content of this booklet could not have been written five years ago: if it requires substantial modification a few years hence current archaeological work in the city will have been a success.

Introduction

Lincoln stands where the belt of limestone known as the Jurassic Ridge is cut by the River Witham. The modern city is dominated by the triple towers of its medieval cathedral and its ancient buildings, its winding streets and the remains of its Roman defences serve as a reminder that the city has a distinguished past spanning at least two thousand years.

For much of this long period archaeological evidence is our only source of information. Over the years many fragments of ancient buildings and objects of antiquity have come to light by chance but it was only in 1945 that archaeological work under professional direction was organized, under the aegis of the Lincoln Archaeological Research Committee. By 1970 major redevelopment schemes proposed for the lower part of the city likely to affect all periods of the city's buried past, created in Lincoln an archaeological crisis similar to those experienced by many other historic centres, and on a massive scale. Modern methods of construction which use deeply-piled foundations and large earth-moving machinery may seriously damage or totally destroy the material remains of successive centuries, but at the same time the clearance of these areas prior to redevelopment can offer unrepeatable opportunities for archaeological investigation. To meet this challenge the Lincoln Archaeological Trust was established in April 1972 and a full-time qualified staff was appointed to undertake excavations in the city and to carry out research on the discoveries for their publication.

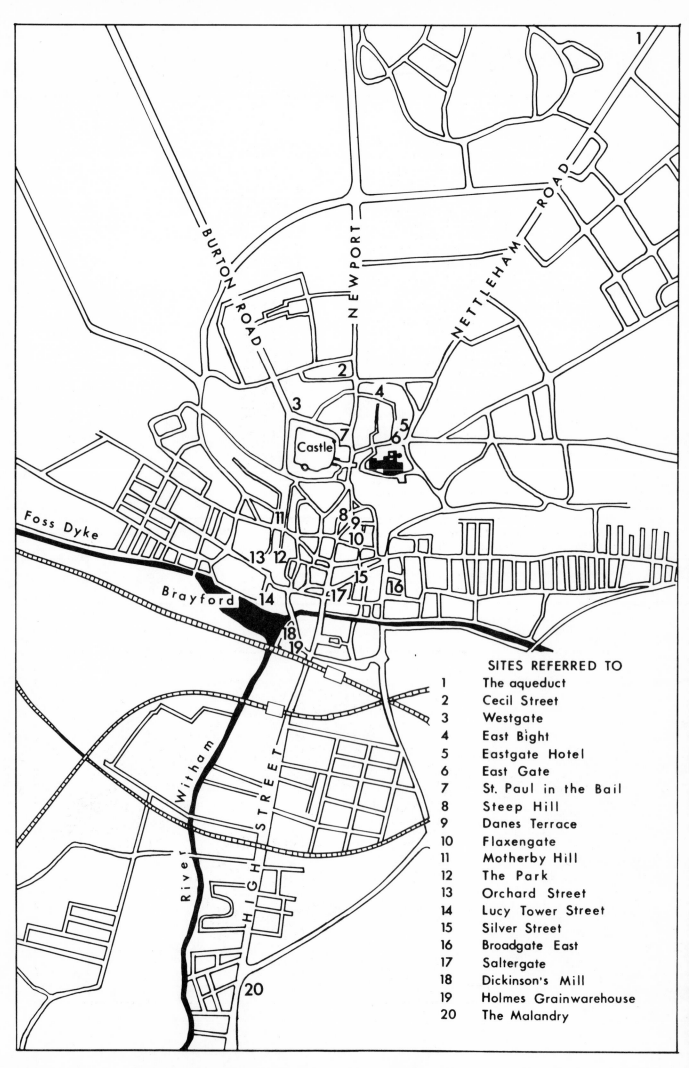

SITES REFERRED TO

1   The aqueduct
2   Cecil Street
3   Westgate
4   East Bight
5   Eastgate Hotel
6   East Gate
7   St. Paul in the Bail
8   Steep Hill
9   Danes Terrace
10 Flaxengate
11 Motherby Hill
12 The Park
13 Orchard Street
14 Lucy Tower Street
15 Silver Street
16 Broadgate East
17 Saltergate
18 Dickinson's Mill
19 Holmes Grainwarehouse
20 The Malandry

Prehistoric Lincoln

The history of the city in the centuries before the Roman conquest is still largely obscure. Prehistoric artefacts typical of cultures covering a vast date-span have been found in Lincoln – a paleolithic handaxe, arrowheads, scrapers, spearheads – all divorced from their original context, churned up and redeposited in the debris of later periods. The hilltop itself commanding the wide surrounding flat lands would probably have attracted early settlement, but relatively little excavation has taken place here apart from work on the Roman defences, and that usually on a limited scale.

The River Witham and the Brayford Pool must also have been focal points in the prehistoric landscape of Lincoln – indeed the first syllable of the modern word 'Lincoln', as of its Roman predecessor *Lindum*, refers to the pool, being derived from the old British word for water, cognate with the Welsh *llyn*, a lake. So it did not come altogether as a surprise when the remains of a settlement of the pre-Roman Iron Age which could well date back as far as the second century B.C., were discovered in 1972 during excavations on the site of Holmes Grainwarehouse, lying between the eastern bank of the Brayford Pool and High Street, opposite the church of St. Mary-le-Wigford. Here were found pottery and other objects of pre-Roman Iron Age type, some excavated from the habitation levels contemporary with a prehistoric ditch and the remains of buildings. A circular drainage gully delimited the position of a native hut, and nearby lay a rectilinear timber building indicated by discolourations in the soil marking the position where timber posts had once been. These are the only structural remains found so far in Lincoln of the Coritani, the tribe which inhabited the region.

Above: one of the brooches in fashion around the time of the Roman invasion of Britain. This example, a Langton Down type, has traces of silvering on the ribbed bow and was found at Holmes Grainwarehouse.   Scale 2:1

Below: sherds of Iron Age pottery from the site at Holmes Grainwarehouse. The piece on the right has been decorated with a burnished curvilinear design.

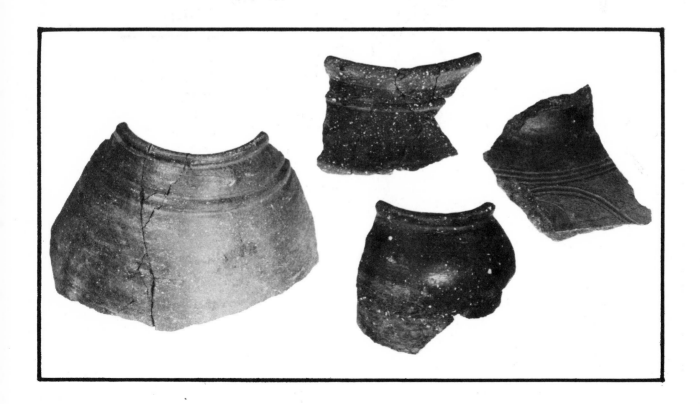

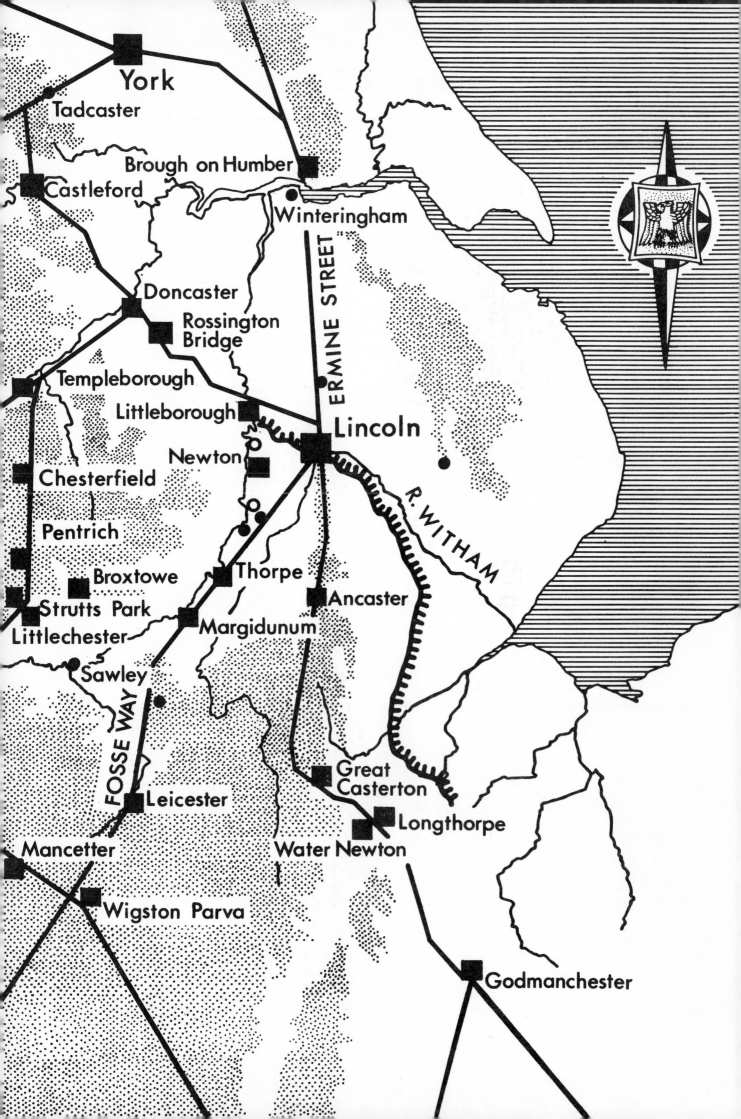

York
Tadcaster
Brough on Humber
Castleford
Winteringham
Doncaster
Rossington Bridge
ERMINE STREET
Templeborough
Littleborough
Lincoln
Newton
Chesterfield
R. WITHAM
Pentrich
Thorpe
Broxtowe
Ancaster
Strutts Park
Margidunum
Littlechester
Sawley
FOSSE WAY
Great Casterton
Leicester
Longthorpe
Mancetter
Water Newton
Wigston Parva
Godmanchester

The Roman army in Lincoln

The legions, the crack troops of the Roman army, were based in fortresses normally sited at the rear of the frontier zone, protected by smaller bases (forts) held by the more expendable auxiliary troops. The considerable strategic potential of Lincoln's geographical position was recognised when the road system was extended to link the network of forts, for it became the pivot of road and water communications. The site controlled the river-crossing at the point where the Witham flows through the limestone ridge to the Wash, and here two major Roman roads met. About a mile and a half south of the river, the main route northwards up the eastern side of Britain, Ermine Street, was joined by the Fosse Way, a diagonal route across lowland Britain linking Lincoln and Exeter. So long as the Brigantes, the powerful northern tribe which occupied lands as far south as the Peak District, remained unconquered and of dubious allegiance, Lincoln held a key position in Roman frontier arrangements.

Early Roman military sites in the East Midlands (opposite):	
Legionary fortress	■
Other forts	■
Possible fort	●
Marching camp	○
Areas of upland	░
Canal – Fosse Dyke to the west of Lincoln, Car Dyke to the east	

The North arrow incorporates the eagle standard (aquila), a symbol which was common to all legions.

The same site at Holmes Grainwarehouse produced fragmentary traces of timber buildings of the early Roman period which may be earlier than the legionary fortress on the hilltop. These discoveries help to emphasise that the history of the Roman military occupation of Lincoln may have been far more complicated than has previously been thought. It should now be viewed in the wider context of changing military dispositions reflecting advancing frontiers and rearward consolidation during the early period of the conquest of Britain. The conquest of the south-east was achieved with some rapidity, but Boudicca's revolt in 60/61 was a major setback affecting military strategy and the siting of individual installations. Likewise the withdrawal from the province of one of its four legions by the Emperor Nero in 66 would have necessitated rationalization of the remaining military forces. These events are likely to have affected Lincoln.

Left: the presence of the Roman army is vividly illustrated by this iron ballista bolt found in the earliest Roman levels at the site of Holmes Grainwarehouse. In the early Roman period there may well have been a military base south of the river.   Scale 1:1

Lincoln has long been recognised as a legionary base. Items of military equipment have been found here, and of the twenty or so inscribed tombstones found in the city, five commemorate soldiers of the Ninth Legion *Hispana* and two are of soldiers of the Second Legion *Adiutrix*, which formed the successive garrisons of the fortress. The hilltop site of the fortress has been identified and the position of its defences confirmed on all four sides. Until recently it was assumed that the Ninth Legion was stationed here from *c.* 48 until it was moved in 71 by the governor Cerialis to build a new base at York for the campaign against the Brigantes. But the position is in fact more complex. Excavations on the site of the north tower of the Roman East Gate (undertaken in the 1960s by Mr. J. B. Whitwell for the Lincoln Archaeological Research Committee) have shown that the hilltop legionary fortress, on the evidence of the pottery dating, was not built until the sixties, a point which has been confirmed by recent work at Westgate and behind the Eastgate Hotel.

The area enclosed by the fortress, roughly forty acres (16 ha.), would not have been sufficient to hold an entire legion; either the legion was depleted or a detachment was based elsewhere. There are indications that in this early period legions were subdivided, sometimes combining with auxiliary troops garrisoned at the same base. Recent work on the site at Longthorpe, near Peterborough, has shown that part of the Ninth Legion was stationed in the Nene Valley between *c.* 48-62 and it has been argued that these detachments moved to Lincoln in the aftermath of Boudicca's rebellion.

Still there are good reasons for believing that there was a Roman military presence in Lincoln before 62. Three of the Lincoln tombstones may be dated on epigraphic grounds to before *c.* 60 as can some of the cremation urns found nearby. Occupation debris pre-dating the building of the fortress was found during excavations on the East Gate (although this could have been connected with preparatory work in laying out the site). In addition an early building of military type has been found at Silver Street (during excavations carried out by the Department of the Environment in 1973), and early Roman occupation has been found south of the river as mentioned above. It is probable that in the early period a mixed garrison including a detachment of the Ninth Legion was stationed at Lincoln on a site which has yet to be identified, perhaps south of the river. This would help to explain the enigmatic siting of both the junction of Fosse Way with Ermine Street about two miles south of the known legionary fortress, and of the legionary cemetery.

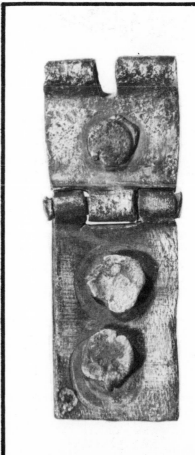

Bronze strap buckle from a legionary's armour. The iron segmental tunic protecting his trunk was held together by hinged straps, which were flexible enough to allow a certain amount of freedom of movement. Found in the legionary levels under the new extension to the Eastgate Hotel at East Bight in 1971.
Scale 5:2

Most of the buildings inside the fortress would have been constructed of timber. This fragment of burnt daub from a legionary building has wattle impressions. Scale 3:4

The disposition of the buildings within the earth and timber defences of the legionary fortress is at present unknown. It is probable that like the later *colonia* the fortress faced east, so that the modern street of Eastgate follows approximately the line of the *via praetoria*, and Bailgate the line of the *via principalis*. A small excavation carried out recently in the grounds of Westgate School revealed a fragment of a legionary building probably best interpreted as part of the centurion's quarters of a barrack-block. Unfortunately much of this area was later used as a stone quarry. Current excavations should reveal part of the headquarters building (*principia*), and other excavations are planned in the vicinity. It is possible that a legionary bath-building may have been incorporated into the *colonia* baths found in 1956–58 at Cottesford Place. The other buildings, such as barrack-blocks, officers' houses, workshops and store-buildings, remain to be found. The plan attempts to combine what is known about the layout of the fortress at present with what may reasonably be conjectured. Little else can be said about the military occupation of Lincoln without further excavations in the city.

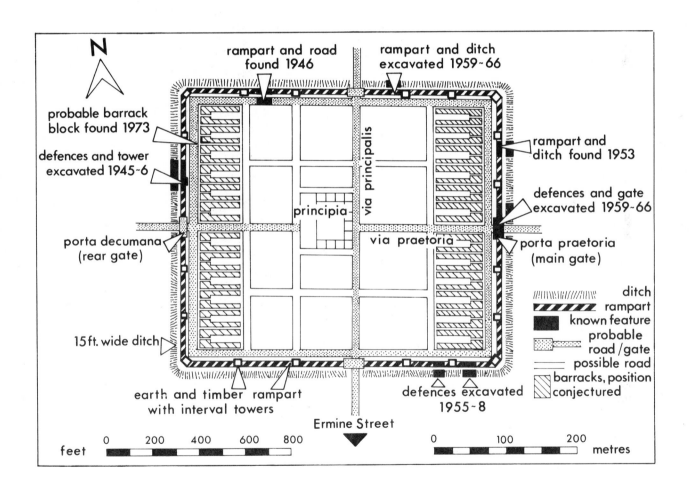

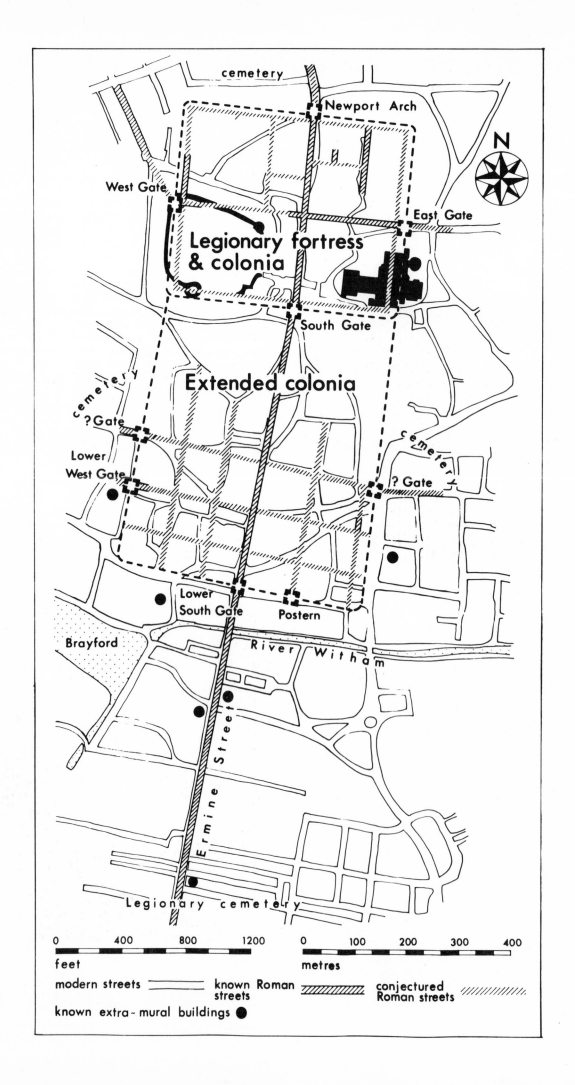

cemetery

Newport Arch

N

West Gate

East Gate

Legionary fortress & colonia

South Gate

cemetery

Extended colonia

?Gate

cemetery

Lower West Gate

? Gate

Lower South Gate

Postern

Brayford

River Witham

Ermine Street

Legionary cemetery

0	400	800	1200

feet

0	100	200	300	400

metres

modern streets —————   known Roman streets //////   conjectured Roman streets //////

known extra-mural buildings ●

The Roman *colonia*

With the pacification of south-eastern Britain and the advance of the Roman frontier, the legion based at Lincoln moved on. As at Gloucester the Roman authorities decided to make use of the area of the fortress by founding a *colonia* on the same site; this happened at Lincoln during the reign of the Emperor Domitian (A.D. 81–96).

Above: the Emperor Domitian portrayed on an as *minted in 87 and found at The Park in a rubbish pit. The* colonia *at Lincoln was probably founded in the closing years of his reign. Scale 3:1*

Although *coloniae* were essentially self-governing communities of Roman citizens their foundation in newly-acquired provinces during the first and second centuries had quasi-military implications. They were seen as bulwarks of Romanization designed to impart Roman customs to recently conquered peoples, and they were inhabited principally by retired legionary veterans, all of whom were Roman citizens. In the classical world the concept of civilization was focused on the idea of the city. Roman cities were vehicles of Roman ideas and culture, and a *colonia*, with the highest status awarded to a provincial city, became a model whose imitation by native peoples was encouraged.

The foundation of a *colonia* at Lincoln was no doubt partly a matter of administrative convenience. *Coloniae* required the apportionment of surrounding lands for their inhabitants, and the Roman army had already acquired this territory when the legionary fortress was established. Excavation has shown that the legionary defences here were not slighted, suggesting continuity of occupation between the withdrawal of the legion and the foundation of the *colonia*, perhaps in the form of a caretaker garrison. The *colonia* at Lincoln flourished; its citizens were Roman citizens, its laws and institutions were modelled closely on those of Rome; the arrangement

of its buildings and streets followed Roman ideas of town-planning, and it produced outstanding examples of Roman provincial sculpture. As Sir Ian Richmond noted thirty years ago, "Roman Lincoln itself offers a glimpse of flourishing Roman urban culture in imported purity such as has not yet emerged anywhere else on British provincial soil".

When the *colonia* was founded, the timber front of the legionary rampart was replaced by a narrow stone wall. Small stone turrets at regular intervals were added to the rear of the wall, and later the legionary earthen bank was heightened. The street system was laid out on a grid pattern, probably influenced in part by the position of the streets of the fortress. It is still not possible to reconstruct the entire street layout, but some if not all of the major streets had elaborate sewers beneath them large enough for a boy to walk in. Knowledge of the buildings within the *colonia* is fragmentary indeed. Most of the recorded remains, including many fine mosaic pavements, give some idea of the quality of life in the *colonia*, but as they have been discovered by chance rather than by systematic excavation their date and function are imperfectly known. The Roman city was in existence for over three hundred years and what has come to

Above: front of the colonia *wall at Cecil Street on the northern defences built over the rammed infill of the legionary ditch. Most of the facing-stones have been removed by later stone-robbers. Note the putlog holes left by the beams to hold the scaffolding of the Roman builders.*

light is not necessarily representative of the *colonia* when it was first established. It is possible that, as at Gloucester, the early inhabitants of the *colonia* lived in buildings which closely resembled the barrack-block accommodation to which they had been accustomed. Only later in the second century did the Gloucester colonists live in more elegant town houses.

No doubt further excavation will show whether this was the case at Lincoln.

Public buildings of stone following classical proto-types would have been provided from the outset. Foremost among these would have been the *forum* complex and the buildings around it, which embodied the Roman ideal of a self-governing community.

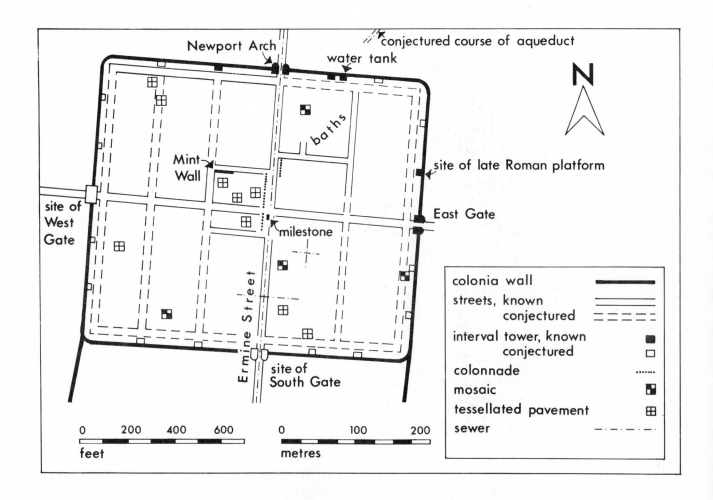

The *forum* itself, the market-place and civic centre, was the hub of urban life. Adjacent were public buildings where the town council met, local administration was conducted and justice was dispensed. The site of the *forum* at Lincoln is still in doubt but it would have been centrally placed. It may have stood on the east side of Bailgate where an *insula* (a city block of buildings within the grid of streets) of slightly larger size than other Lincoln examples apparently existed. Alternatively the *forum* could have lain opposite, on the west side of Ermine Street partly beneath the now demolished church of St. Paul-in-the-Bail where excavations are currently in progress. Here along the Ermine Street frontage stood the colonnade of a building complex of classical proportions and monumental scale. Some of the column bases survive in cellars of existing properties along Bailgate and the position where others were found in the late nine-teenth century is marked out in granite setts in the modern street-surface. Part of the north wall of this remarkable range of buildings survives to a height of about 18 ft. (5.5m.) at the rear of the old North District School in Westgate and is known as the Mint Wall. The prospect of exciting discoveries nearby beneath the succession of ecclesiastical buildings at St. Paul seems certain.

A magnificent public bath-house situated inside the northern defences east of Ermine Street was excavated at Cottesford Place in 1956–58. Other public buildings including theatre, amphitheatre and temples await discovery, and detailed archaeological work is needed to establish the development of the typical shops and houses of the *colonia*.

Roman Lincoln needed a water-supply sufficient to flush its sewers, to service its bath-house, and to fulfil other domestic and commercial needs. The source of an aqueduct pipeline and its course along the Nettleham Road were investigated during the 1950s. Members of the Society for Lincolnshire History and Archaeology are currently attempting to establish where the aqueduct entered the *colonia*. A clue has recently been found at East Bight. Here the base of what is thought to have been a water-tower (*castellum aquae*) lying just inside the northern defences of the *colonia* has been partially uncovered. Its massive foundations and the presence of *opus signinum* (cement used in the lining of the tank) help to distinguish it from other towers of defensive purpose. If this identification is correct its siting near the bath-house would be explained.

Fieldwork and excavation in the 1950s confirmed the source of the aqueduct at the Roaring Meg springs and much of its course along the Nettleham Road. Recent development along its line enabled the Trust to expose and lift a stretch of the pipeline at a point where it was below ground-level.

Defences of the colonia *exposed at East Bight, showing the base of an interval-tower in the foreground and an upstanding section of rebuilt wide* colonia *wall. To the right of the tower lie the remains of what was probably a water-tank. This was built before the* colonia *wall was widened, and the overhang visible on the rear side of the widened wall accommodated its shape.*

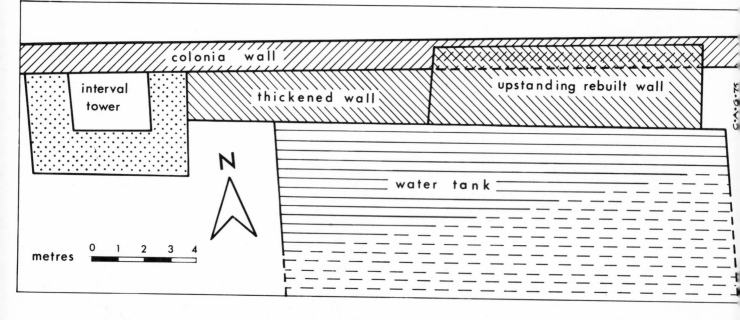

Burial within the walls of a city was forbidden by ancient Roman law and Lincoln, like other cities, had extensive cemeteries outside its walls, especially alongside the roads leading from its gates. Two cremation burials were found at The Park pre-dating the defences on the hillside. One, in the reconstructed black-burnished cooking pot (right) seems to have been marked out by a small structure carried on four stakes. It is interesting to note that the areas of burning occur on the lower part of the vessel exactly where one would expect to find them on a normal cooking pot, suggesting that perhaps it had been used for cooking before receiving the cremation! The pot stands 7 ins. high.

The lower Roman city

Although both the legionary fortress and the *colonia* which soon replaced it were confined by their defences to the hilltop, the hillside to the south sloping down to the Witham was also occupied from the early Roman period. Settlement here would have originated in temporary trading-stalls (*canabae*) set up to serve the needs of the legion, and the line of Ermine Street itself seems to have attracted ribbon-development. By *c*.200 the hillside was considered important enough to warrant its enclosure within defences which extended down from the upper *colonia* to the northern margins of the river.

Recently several major excavations have taken place in this lower part of the city, prompted by large-scale redevelopment. Several sites provided an opportunity to investigate the defences: The Park and West Parade (Motherby Hill) on the western side, Saltergate on the southern line, and the Broadgate edge of the Silver Street site on the eastern defences. When several major sites became available for excavation in 1973 the Department of the Environment helped to relieve the pressure on the Trust by investigating the last two sites mentioned.

The discoveries made on these four sites have not only helped to elucidate the complex sequence of the defences but have also provided information about the layout and development of the area they enclosed. At The Park fragmentary remains of at least nine Roman buildings of different periods were found underlying the defences. Superimposed traces of five of these were found beneath the wide fourth-century rampart, dating from the second half of the first century to the third century. Of these the four earliest phases of building were of timber construction and only slight traces remained; they underlay another building whose timber walls were based on stone sills. Other structures included a substantial second-century stone building with exceptionally deep foundations. All the buildings discovered at The Park were regularly laid out either parallel or at right-angles to Ermine Street and the line followed by the extended *colonia* wall.

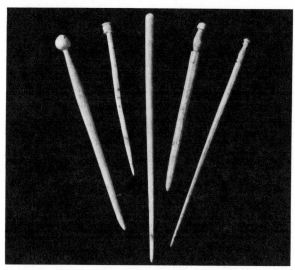

A selection of bone pins, a few of the many excavated at The Park. These were commonly used as clothes-fasteners and some were probably hair pins. Found among a huge dump of Roman rubbish deposited to help increase the size of the late Roman rampart.

Buildings had also existed on the course later followed by the eastern defences. The earliest structure found on the site excavated here (Silver Street) was a timber building whose plan resembled that of a store-building, perhaps a granary. In the later first century there were more timber structures, replaced by a stone building in the early second century which was demolished for the erection of the defences. To judge from the quantities of painted wall plaster which were recovered in the debris of its destruction it had probably been a fine town house. Apart from producing a well-preserved stretch of *colonia* wall, the Saltergate site revealed part of a town house inside the lower city lying on the south side of and continuing beneath modern Silver Street. This had at least three heated rooms with channelled hypocausts and was apparently built in the early fourth century.

During 1974-75 work has concentrated in the main on the excavation of sites near the centre of the extended *colonia*. So far work at Flaxengate and Danes Terrace has been confined to the post-Roman levels, but the presence of Roman walls which survived to a considerable height into the medieval period, and in one case well beyond, augurs well for future discoveries. This particular area provides an opportunity to excavate the greater part of a sample *insula*. Nearby on Steep Hill a small site has recently been excavated north of Jews' Court, and has produced part of a Roman building out of orientation with the street grid. One room had a polychrome tessellated pavement with a border of red and white bands but most of the mosaic had been obliterated by later structures. Terracing created at different periods to facilitate building on the steep slope has created bizarre archaeological stratigraphy on this part of the hillside: Roman floor levels here were higher than their medieval and Victorian counterparts, and even above the level of the modern surface of Steep Hill.

Excavations within the lower town and the discovery of two previously unsuspected gates on its defences have enabled a partial reconstruction of the layout of streets in the lower town to be made. Here also there appears to have been a grid pattern and there are now some indications that the grid may have been laid out at an earlier date than the extended *colonia* defences. On the eastern side, just beyond the tail of the rampart, a street was found running north-south complete with a wooden water-pipe along its western edge. This was not part of an *intervallum* circuit (such as existed in the upper city) since there was no trace of a road in the corresponding position on the western side of the lower *colonia*. There is slight evidence to suggest that part of the gridiron street system was cut off when the extended defences were constructed. On the Broadgate East site outside the lower *colonia* ditch, a fragment of Roman street was found. If this ran east-west, which could not positively be determined, it would have followed the alignment of a street known inside the *colonia* and might once have been continuous with it before being cut into two parts by the imposition of defences. The street pattern on the steeper part of the hillside is still obscure but it may have been related to a system of terracing.

Detailed information has been obtained about the construction of the fortifications around the extended *colonia* and their modification later in the Roman period. Initially they consisted of a narrow stone wall and a compacted sand and clay rampart, formed largely of the material upcast from digging the ditch-system around the outside. Soon afterwards a series of interval-towers was added to the rear of the *colonia* wall. Two have been located on the western defences: one, with massive walls, on Motherby Hill; the other at The Park, in the position later occupied by the Lower West Gate. Both were demolished during the Roman period, that at The Park for the insertion of a new gate in the fourth century. The tower on Motherby Hill may have been replaced in function by the fourth-century construction of a large solid stone structure nearby, tentatively interpreted as a platform to bear the heavy stone-throwing artillery

Consolidating a fragment of mosaic at Steep Hill.

machines in use in the late Roman Empire. There appears to have been a systematic dismantling of interval-towers in Lincoln. In 1971 during emergency excavations behind the Eastgate Hotel in the upper Roman city another tower was discovered. This also had become redundant and its north wall had been levelled in the fourth century to help form the foundations of a solid internal structure resembling the platform found on Motherby Hill.

Late Roman flagon, 9½ ins. high made from a pale red-brown clay, with bronze colour-coating. Flagons are much rarer towards the end of the Roman period, but colour-coated flagons with pinched necks occur in the major late industries. No exact parallel has been found for this example; it may prove to be the product of a local kiln producing colour-coated wares in the later fourth century yet to be discovered. Complete vessels are rare finds outside a burial context. This was found inside an oven at The Park along with a complete chicken's egg, the skeleton of a small bird and mussel shells. The oven had been built late in the fourth century in the angle between the north gate-tower and the re-built colonia *wall.*

The base of the interval-tower on Motherby Hill, showing its massive walls which were perhaps designed in part to buttress the colonia *wall on the steep slope. Its lowest floor would have been at a higher level than any of the surviving masonry. In the foreground are medieval structures built from the tower's masonry.*

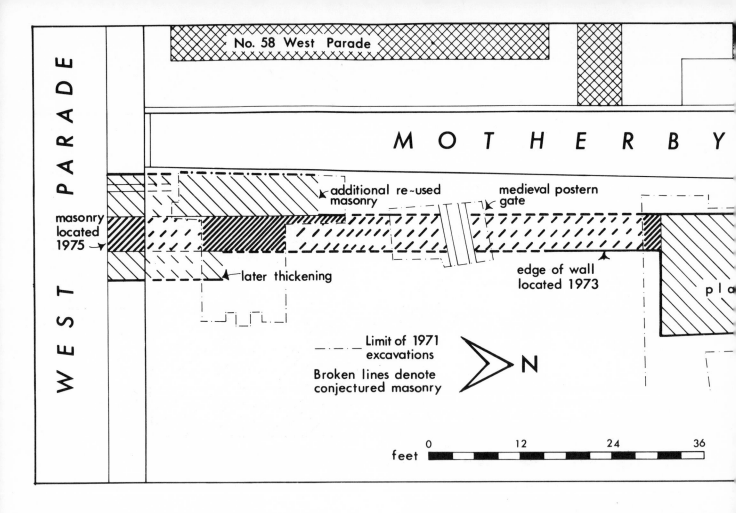

No. 58 West Parade

WEST PARADE

MOTHERBY

masonry located 1975 →

← additional re-used masonry

medieval postern gate

← later thickening

edge of wall located 1973

pla

─ ─ · ─ Limit of 1971 excavations

Broken lines denote conjectured masonry

N

0   12   24   36

feet

At about the same time the *colonia* wall, the rampart and the ditch were refurbished. Some sections of the wall were completely demolished and replaced by a wider wall. One example of a rebuilt stretch can be seen at The Park (north of the gate-towers), and another at Saltergate, near the Falcon Inn. The rebuilding of the southern line could not be closely dated, but at The Park it was certainly constructed in the second half of the fourth century.

At various points on the defences around the lower city, the original narrow wall continued in use, sometimes strengthened by additional masonry inserted against its rear face. Localized thickenings occurred immediately north of the interval-tower on Motherby Hill and at the southern end of the site. A fine example of thickened wall south of the gateway at The Park has been consolidated and is permanently on display. Also at the southern end of Motherby Hill large blocks of re-used masonry were added to the front of the wall, perhaps forming part of a tower of the gate thought to have existed at this point.

At The Park extraordinary circumstances made possible the excavation of the total width of the defences, from the outer lip of the ditch to beyond the tail of the rampart. The ditch system was found to have been recut in the late Roman period, providing the city with a ditch some 80 ft. (*c*.25m.) wide. The rampart, refurbished on a similar scale, was heightened and widened.

It is unlikely that a ditch was dug outside the southern line of the *colonia* wall, presumably on account of the proximity of the river. Observations made in 1971 during the laying of services across Newland established the presence of a street, a point that has been confirmed by work at Saltergate.

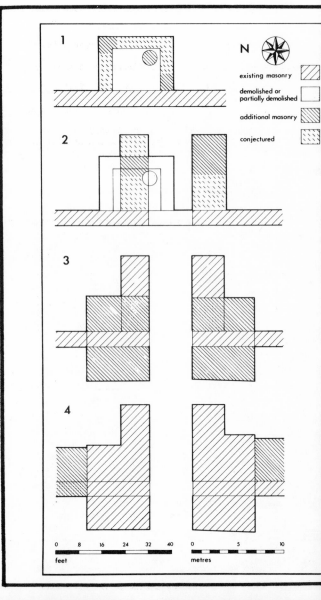

N

existing masonry

demolished or partially demolished

additional masonry

conjectured

1

2

3

4

0   8   16   24   32   40
feet

0   5   10
metres

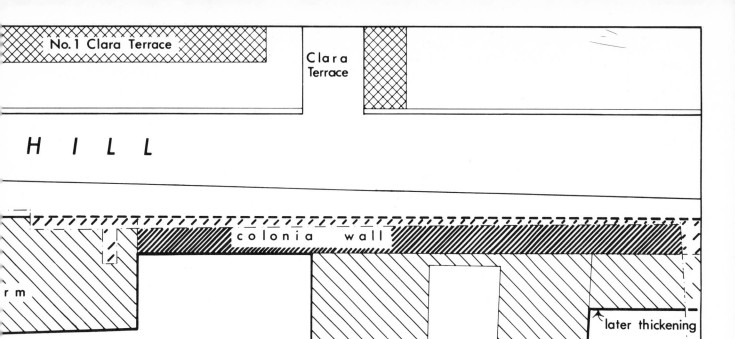

No. 1 Clara Terrace

Clara Terrace

H I L L

r m

colonia wall

later thickening

interval tower

0   5   10   metres

Left: schematic plan showing the phases of defensive masonry at The Park.
1. *An interval-tower with a well was added to the* colonia *wall (probably early third century).*
2. *A gateway with internally-projecting walls flanking the roadway replaced the interval-tower.*
3. *The fourth-century gateway with rectangular towers was built incorporating earlier masonry.*
4. *Soon afterwards the* colonia *wall was rebuilt north of the gate and to the south the existing wall was thickened on the inside.*

Below: plan of the Lower West Gate at The Park. Stretches of the colonia *wall were incorporated into the fourth-century gate-towers, the bases of which were chiefly formed of stone re-used from an earlier building. The towers were originally L-shaped in plan and were hollow to accommodate guard-chambers. The walls projecting eastwards on either side of the roadway revetted the rampart and perhaps once contained staircases up into the guard-chambers. The rear of the guard-chambers at first-floor level, including fragments of the floors, survive: the rest was demolished when houses were built along The Park in the 1840s and the bases of the gate-towers were used as cellar floors.*

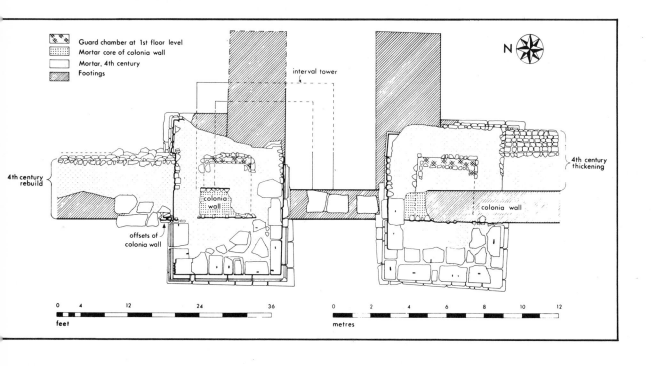

N

▨ Guard chamber at 1st floor level
▦ Mortar core of colonia wall
☐ Mortar, 4th century
▨ Footings

interval tower

4th century thickening

4th century rebuild

colonia wall

colonia wall

offsets of colonia wall

0   4   12   24   36
feet

0   2   4   6   8   10   12
metres

ate Roman defences at The Park.

Above: the fourth-century gateway at The Park from the west. The gate-towers were hollow to accommodate guard-chambers. The road surfaces have been removed by the excavations and beneath lie the foundations of the colonia wall.

Left: the base of the north gate-tower built around the truncated colonia wall and incorporating many re-used architectural fragments.

Right: details of the re-used masonry.

4. *Above: north of the gate the colonia wall was rebuilt in the second half of the fourth century. No attempt had been made to face the bottom of the wall, but the top courses were roughly-faced and neatly mortared. The rampart stood to the top of the surviving masonry.*

5. *Left: the late fourth-century strengthening added to the rear of the colonia wall extended only for 52 ft. (15.8m.) south of the gate. The superstructure was built in short stretches getting narrower towards the south. Its overall width at base was 16 ft. (4.9m.). Further south the colonia wall had been demolished and replaced by a new wall 10 ft. (c. 3m.) wide.*

6. *Above: back of the south gate-tower and the thickened* colonia *wall from the east. None of the surviving masonry was visible in the Roman period when it was covered by the earth rampart.*

7. *Right: rear of the north gate-tower; the facing stones had been robbed out in the thirteenth century.*

8. *Right: removal of a re-used decorated cornice-moulding which had been built upside down into the base of the north gate-tower. The original has now been replaced with a cast.*

9. *Below: detail of the decoration. Photograph by T. F. C. Blagg.*

Left: solid internal platform on the eastern defences of the upper town, now beneath extensions to the Eastgate Hotel. It was constructed over the demolished north wall of an interval-tower.

Below: internal platform at Motherby Hill, partly excavated and now lying beneath the Divisional Police Headquarters. On the right is the inner face of the colonia wall.

Excavations were carried out by the Department of the Environment at Saltergate on the
southern defences of the lower town.
Above: remains of a postern-gate,
Below: rear of the rebuilt colonia wall with medieval masonry built on top.

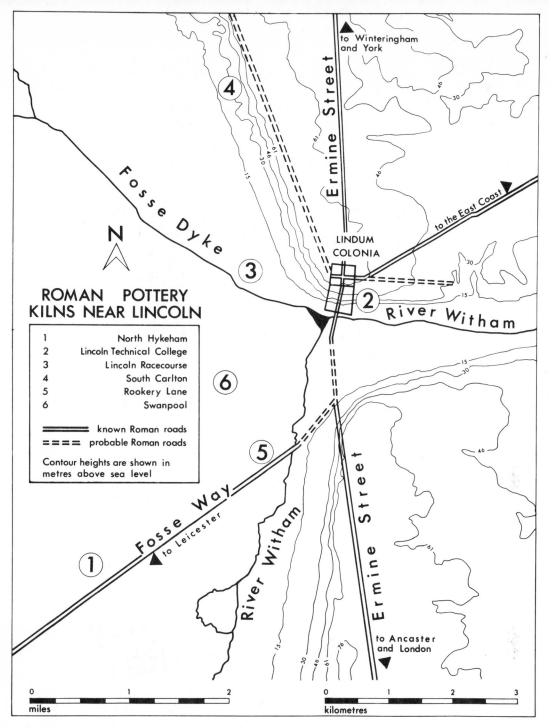

ROMAN POTTERY KILNS NEAR LINCOLN

1	North Hykeham
2	Lincoln Technical College
3	Lincoln Racecourse
4	South Carlton
5	Rookery Lane
6	Swanpool

known Roman roads
probable Roman roads

Contour heights are shown in metres above sea level

Lincoln was well supplied with pottery from local kilns throughout the Roman period, the kilns ranging in date from the late first century through to the fourth century and situated in the outlying areas of the city. As yet the kilns of the pottery occurring in legionary levels at Lincoln have not been located. The products of the kilns are of great interest, illustrating the range of vessels in use at various periods at Lincoln, and include kitchen wares, drinking vessels, flagons and *mortaria* (mixing bowls) in varying fabrics and designs, dependent on the kiln date and siting. Of particular interest are the kilns at South Carlton which produced fine wares in a white fabric derived from an iron-free clay, often colour-coated light red and also painted in a variety of designs. Moreover, it was this kiln which "exported" *mortaria* to the northern frontier of Roman Britain, where examples stamped with the names of the South Carlton potters have been found on Hadrian's Wall and the Antonine Wall. *Mortaria* from the Technical College Kiln were also exported, though the distribution of its products appears to have been more limited, extending north into Yorkshire with one example possibly from this kiln occurring at the Roman fort at Newstead, north of Hadrian's Wall.

This "exportation" of *mortaria* has added interest in that these vessels were also brought into Lincoln throughout the Roman period, particularly from the Midlands kilns of Hartshill and Mancetter (Warwicks.), and also from the Nene Valley. *Mortaria* from the latter area may well have been transported up the Car Dyke to Lincoln in consignments of pottery which also included the well-known barbotine-decorated beakers of "Castor ware", some cups decorated with hunting scenes. This abnormality regarding *mortaria* may suggest that the South Carlton potters had obtained contracts for the supply of pottery to the army of the North, and were not principally employed in supplying *mortaria* to the civilian population in and around Lincoln. Pottery from the major late pottery-producing centres at Swanpool and Rookery Lane turns up in quantity during the excavation of all late Roman deposits at Lincoln, the Swanpool kilns in particular making a very wide range of vessels and clearly supplying the city's requirements fairly fully.

(This note on the Roman pottery kilns in the Lincoln area has been supplied by Miss M. J. Darling, Roman Pottery Researcher for the Lincoln Archaeological Trust, working with the aid of a grant from the Leverhulme Trust).

The suburbs

The occupation of Roman Lincoln was not confined to the land enclosed by its walls. There was suburban settlement at all periods characterized by ribbon-development alongside the main roads leading from the city. This seems to have been particularly extensive to the south along Ermine Street, where remains of several buildings are known; one, a fine house with mosaic pavements, lay over half a mile from the south gate of the lower *colonia*.

The area south of the river has a complex history which may be illustrated by the discoveries made on the Holmes Grainwarehouse site. Apart from the prehistoric and early Roman timber buildings mentioned above, three periods of stone buildings were excavated, fronting on to Ermine Street. The earliest of these, constructed *c.* 100, extended back at least 90 ft. (27 m.) from the street and is unlikely to have been domestic in function. Part of one of its walls was incorporated into an enigmatic building which replaced it towards the end of the second century. This curious building was elliptical in plan, its stone walls were covered with wall plaster and its floor with clay. In the fourth century it was replaced by a substantial building with a cellar, which in the fifteenth century was re-used as a cess-pit.

Little excavation has taken place outside the western defences of the city. The few discoveries made outside the ditch near the Lower West Gate suggest a sequence of timber and stone buildings. Rescue excavations on a larger scale did, however, take place east of Broadgate at a corresponding point outside the eastern defences. The area did not appear to have been densely occupied in the Roman period but detailed investigation was confined to the northern part of the site. Fragmentary remains of timber buildings dating to the early second century were found. These were replaced later in the second century by a stone house which subsequently received a baths-suite. The cold room (*frigidarium*) was well preserved. Iron slag and furnaces were indicative of industrial activity in the vicinity, perhaps associated with the timber buildings.

The material remains found in recent excavations, especially the massive late Roman defences, tend to reflect the city's importance in the late Roman period, and perhaps reinforce the suggestion that Lincoln was one of the new provincial capitals when Britain was sub-divided into four provinces as part of the late Roman reorganisation of the Western Empire.

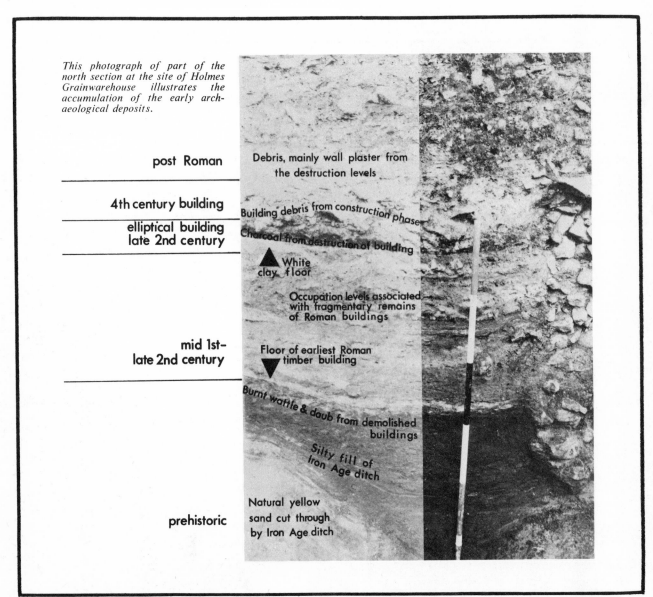

This photograph of part of the north section at the site of Holmes Grainwarehouse illustrates the accumulation of the early archaeological deposits.

post Roman

4th century building

elliptical building
late 2nd century

mid 1st–
late 2nd century

prehistoric

Debris, mainly wall plaster from the destruction levels

Building debris from construction phase

Charcoal from destruction of building

White clay floor

Occupation levels associated with fragmentary remains of Roman buildings

Floor of earliest Roman timber building

Burnt wattle & daub from demolished buildings

Silty fill of Iron Age ditch

Natural yellow sand cut through by Iron Age ditch

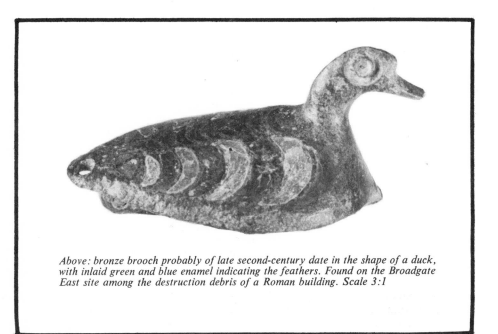

Above: bronze brooch probably of late second-century date in the shape of a duck, with inlaid green and blue enamel indicating the feathers. Found on the Broadgate East site among the destruction debris of a Roman building. Scale 3:1

Below: cold plunge-bath uncovered at Broadgate East. The bath was lined with cement and had been damaged by medieval rubbish pits.

Lincoln between the Romans & Danes

Belt-buckle found at The Park in 1968, of a type worn in the later fourth century possibly by a soldier. Scale 2:1 (City and County Museum)

Recent archaeological discoveries have provided information about some aspects of life in the city during the closing years of the Roman administration. The picture is of material prosperity and political insecurity. At The Park, the refurbishing of the fortifications and the discovery (by the Lincoln Archaeological Research Committee) of a type of belt-buckle usually considered one of the trappings of the late fourth-century militia, illustrate the late Roman policies of strengthening town defences against attack and presumably of garrisoning troops within them. Stylistically the buckle displays Germanic influence. Lincoln's late Roman cemeteries seem the major potential source of information about the make up of the population of the city at this period, and are as yet untapped.

Although the archaeological evidence from this country is still inadequate, the fate of major Roman towns during the fifth and six centuries is now becoming clearer. The cities of the Empire had depended upon the Roman economic and social structure, and the collapse of the Roman administration brought about the disintegration of the economy and of the existing social order. The settlement of Germanic peoples of a quite different cultural background helped to accelerate the process, for urban life was not an intrinsic element in the structure of Anglo-Saxon society. Nevertheless it is clear that although some Roman towns may have been abandoned, others, notably London and York, continued to be occupied. Several further Roman cities have now produced evidence for Anglo-Saxon settlement at an early date within their walls, but the subsequent history of the original citizens and their relationship to the newcomers is more difficult for archaeologists to trace. Generally the picture is one of drastic decline in population and evident deterioration in material standards. What had been flourishing urban centres clearly declined during this time to settlements in most cases of no more than village status.

The paucity of contemporary documentation for the fifth and sixth centuries and the confused, often conflicting, accounts of later writers make every fragment of archaeological information for this period of paramount importance. This evidence is slight and exceptionally difficult to recover and interpret. In Lincoln the evidence of modern scientific excavation does not reinforce the once current impression that the Roman city ended in a holocaust of fire and slaughter, yet undoubtedly the changes were profound, if more gradual. A meagre but increasing body of evidence suggests that part of the area enclosed by the defences continued in occupation and that civic activity extended into the early part of the fifth century. It is reasonable to suppose that only certain quarters of what had been the Roman city were inhabited, and that certain Roman buildings, or parts of them, continued in use. Roman buildings at Flaxengate and on the north side of the Saltergate site were still standing and in use around the time of the Norman Conquest. Although direct proof is lacking, it is possible that they may have continued in use throughout the Saxon period.

The archaeological evidence from Lincoln is far from conclusive. The absence both of a circulating coinage and, apparently, of pottery for domestic use deprives us of the precise dating methods applicable to the Roman period when dealing with the occupation deposits and fragments of timber buildings stratigraphically assignable to these centuries. Very few examples of the characteristic pagan Saxon metalwork have been found at Lincoln, and none in a context to which structural remains might be related with certainty.

Further information is urgently needed about this period, so important for a fuller understanding of Lincoln's historical development. It is hoped that more light will be thrown on these years by current work on two sites of great potential importance, St. Paul-in-the-Bail and Flaxengate. The relatively rare dedications to St. Paul are normally thought to be early, and tradition assigns an early date to the establishment of a church to St. Paul on the Bailgate site. Lying as it does within a monumental building-complex whose north wall still stands, presumably because it was in constant use, it is tempting to suggest that the site of the later church came to have Christian associations in the later Roman period and that the prestigious Roman buildings in their key position at the centre of the upper Roman town attracted the early kings of Lindsey. The potential importance of the Flaxengate site lies in its relationship to the Roman road system. Excavations are being conducted at the junction of two Roman roads, one (on the line of modern Grantham Street) probably the main east-west route across the lower city, the other (Flaxengate) running north-south and leading to the posterngate on the eastern side of the southern defences.

Here the survival of the alignment of the Roman streets into the medieval period and beyond argues that the routes between the gates continued to be used, and the results of work on the site to date indicate that evidence of occupation here in the pagan Saxon or early Christian periods may be forthcoming.

The Venerable Bede, writing from Northumbria a century later, provides tantalizing information about Lincoln in the early seventh century in his narrative about the conversion to Christianity of the pagan Anglo-Saxon kingdoms. Lincoln lay within the kingdom of Lindsey, but apart from the name of its kings little is known about the royal dynasty and nothing of the location of its palaces. At the time of the events which Bede describes, Lindsey was apparently under the overlordship of King Edwin of Northumbria. Bede relates how Bishop Paulinus of York, having converted the Northumbrian royal house, came first to Lincoln in his mission to spread Christianity to Lindsey. Here he was met by a man called Blecca whom Bede describes as *praefectus civitatis*, some sort of civic official or reeve. Paulinus converted Blecca and his household and "a beautiful stone church"

was built in Lincoln, the earliest in Lindsey. Here shortly afterwards Honorius was consecrated fifth Archbishop of Canterbury, and because of its associations the church was held in great reverence and miracles were said to have been performed there. Bede adds that in his own day the church had lost its roof, but he does not know how this had come about.

Excavations in progress at St. Paul-in-the-Bail.

A drawing dated 1784 by S. H. Grimm shows Old St. Paul's church. It was rebuilt c. 1300 incorporating an earlier tower. Photograph by courtesy of Lincolnshire Museums. (Usher Gallery).

The Georgian church, built in 1786.

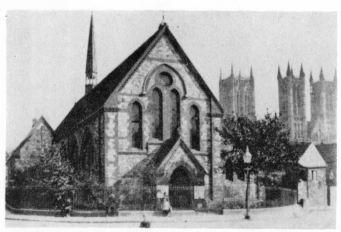

The Victorian church, built in 1877-79 and demolished in 1971.

Bede's narrative poses a legion of questions. Did Paulinus choose Lincoln as the place from which to launch his mission in Lindsey because it was the chief centre of Lindsey in his own day, or from a dim remembrance of its Roman past perpetuated by its massive defences? The presence of an official in Lincoln implies that there was some sort of political organisation. Whose authority did he represent? Was he, as seems likely, a royal official? Why was Paulinus' church roofless a century later? Was this an accidental or localised change in fortune, while generally Christian worship continued to flourish in Lincoln, or did the unsettled times, perhaps specifically the growth of Mercian hegemony, affect the prosperity and spiritual centres of Lincoln? Although the wider issues may never be fully understood, the excavation of the site at St. Paul-in-the-Bail, which tradition associates with the earliest church in Lindsey, should show whether Paulinus' church stood here, and provide valuable information about the early development of ecclesiastical buildings in the city.

By providing a centre here for proselytizing activities in the surrounding area the introduction of Christianity may have accelerated the growth of Lincoln as a community. New focal points within Lincoln would have been created by the establishment of places for Christian worship as well as by the presence of royal interests, so that gradually much of the Roman gridiron of streets came to be irrelevant But the legacy of Lincoln's Roman defences and the main routes between its ancient gates continued to exert an influence on the physical layout of Lincoln as it changed. Standing remains or crumbling ruins of Roman buildings must also have affected the siting of new buildings; the problems involved in demolition and clearance of Roman stone structures would have been considerable.

Recent excavations have shown that Middle Saxon pottery (c. 650–850) is widely distributed throughout the city, which may be an indication of the growth of the population and the revival of Lincoln during this period. At Saltergate stratified pottery of this type was found associated with timber structures which may tentatively be interpreted as an addition to an extant Roman stone building possibly still in occupation. At The Park several groups were found, some in rubbish pits dug into the top of the Roman rampart, others in deposits impinging on the road through the Lower West Gate. Residual sherds have been found at Broadgate, Flaxengate and Danes Terrace, on the last two sites mentioned upcast from their original context which awaits further archaeological investigation.

Left: A succession of later churches stood on the site of St. Paul-in-the-Bail, which tradition associates with the earliest church in Lincoln.

Lincoln in the Scandinavian period

The earliest Viking attacks on Lindsey are recorded in the annals of 841, but during the second half of the ninth century Viking interests shifted from plundering expeditions to military conquest and settlement. In the East Midlands the Danish armies colonized lands grouped around defensible positions known as *burhs*. In the mid-tenth century the Five Boroughs of Lincoln, Stamford, Derby, Nottingham and Leicester emerged as a well-defined entity within the sphere of Danish influence.

Although the Danish settlers left comparatively few distinctive material remains by which the archaeologist can distinguish them from the rest of the community, their influence can be traced by the art historian and the philologist. The study of personal and place-names shows that the Danish element in Lincoln was considerable: approximately half the names of Lincoln moneyers active between the reigns of King Edgar (959–75) and the later years of Ethelred II (979–1016) were Scandinavian.

Nothing illustrates the revival of economic life in Lincoln so forcefully as the history of its coinage. In the late ninth century, the Danes began to strike coins in the areas under their control, and the mint established in Lincoln produced regular issues of coin from the reign of King Edgar (959–75), attaining a position of importance second only to that at London for much of the later Scandinavian period. There are a few rare issues at Lincoln in the early part of the tenth century when the city was under Scandinavian control. Coinage was circulating in Lincoln early, as a recent find at Flaxengate of a Thetford issue of a St. Edmund penny, struck *c.* 905–10, illustrates. This is the earliest post-Roman coin known to have been found at Lincoln.

The study of the coinage, particularly the detailed work of Professor R. H. M. Dolley, is providing clues to the understanding of the obscure political history of Lincoln in the first half of the tenth century. Another rare coin found at Flaxengate was a penny dated 942–43 of Anlaf (Olaf) Qaran Sihtricsson, the Hiberno-Norse princeling whose kingdom was based on York. This helps to reinforce the other tenuous numismatic evidence that the political and commercial ties between Lindsey and York were perhaps closer than the evidence of the literary sources alone would suggest.

While the numismatist can provide clues to the structure of the population and its political and trading connections, archaeological information drawn from contexts which likewise yield numismatic material is of the utmost importance, as the example of Winchester has so convincingly shown, in evoking the vitality of the late Anglo-Saxon town by providing details about its material traditions and physical development. The site at Flaxengate, currently under excavation, shows signs of marking a breakthrough in the study of the elusive Anglo-Scandinavian period at Lincoln. In association with the remarkable series of tenth- and eleventh-century coins an abundance of pottery of the Anglo-Scandinavian period has been found stratified in an unbroken sequence of occupation since *c.* 900: the coins will provide a framework for the analysis of the development of pottery styles which up to the present have not been dated with any precision.

If there is little archaeological evidence to show the influence of the Danish army on the fortifications of the city, their effect on its economic and commercial life is well attested. On the Flaxengate site there is fascinating evidence of extensive industrial activity during the tenth century involving a number of processes connected with the manufacture of objects of copper alloy. Finds of crucibles indicate that the molten metal was being cast, and numerous offcuts suggest another process using copper alloy sheet. Detailed metallurgical study will provide further information about the raw material and the methods of manufacture. Objects of iron were also being manufactured on the site in the tenth century. Apart from the evidence of industrial activity, fragmentary remains of timber buildings dating from the tenth to the twelfth centuries have been excavated along the Grantham Street frontage. The Flaxengate street surface itself was cobbled in the tenth or early eleventh century but this does not appear to have been maintained and later, at around the time of the Conquest, a property boundary encroached upon it.

The economic prosperity of the city was paralleled by an evident expansion in population, and some areas of Lincoln were settled for the first time. Work at Broadgate East has produced archaeological evidence to support a pre-Conquest origin for the suburb of Butwerk which lay outside the eastern defences of the lower town. Timber buildings were found here along the outer lip of the city ditch and along the western side of Friars Lane.

The evidence of the Domesday Survey, particularly the reference to the demolition of 166 properties to make way for the Conqueror's castle, attests to relatively dense occupation of the upper town, although this need not reflect the settlement pattern of the early Scandinavian period. So far archaeological discoveries of this period have been confined to sites in the lower city. Excavation at a site on Steep Hill adjacent to Jews' Court has shown that part of a late Roman building was remodelled to align with St. Martin's Street, the lane linking Steep Hill with the ancient church of St. Martin. A pre-Conquest date for this building is probable, although dating evidence is inconclusive. Nearby at the corner of Danes Terrace and the Strait excavation has revealed an accumulation of deposits representing the remains of timber buildings during examination of later structures. These await detailed examination but the residual pottery and coins found in later levels are indicative of pre-Conquest occupation here also.

Uncertainty still surrounds the exact location of the *burh* occupied by the Danish army in the early years of their settlement. It is unlikely that the Roman defences were ignored and part, at least, of their circuit was probably re-used, although recent excavations have consistently failed to locate any modifications to them before the thirteenth century, apart perhaps from the blocking of some of the minor gates. The massive late Roman fortifications may have needed no improvement. Yet the river and the Brayford Pool lay outside the Roman defensive system and Lincoln's ideal network of waterways must have played a vital role in the military and commercial activities of the Vikings. There was undoubtedly a shift in the city's centre of gravity towards the river in this period and this is reflected in the growth of the prosperous suburb of Wigford. The Sincil Dyke, which has usually been assumed to be of Roman origin, forms part of the water circuit around Wigford, and its construction could perhaps be assigned more appropriately to the Scandinavian era.

There is good reason to suppose that a large part of the physical pattern of medieval Lincoln emerged at this time. Many of its streets and most of its churches are first mentioned only in later documents but their origins lie in a period for which the documents are largely absent, and represent an aspect of urban history on which surviving written records are silent. It was undoubtedly the Scandinavian era which saw Lincoln develop as a major market and assume its characteristic urban form and shape. In these two centuries before the Norman Conquest Lincoln grew into one of the wealthiest and most populous towns in England.

Below: excavation of the tenth-century levels at Flaxengate showing the cobbled street surface (right), fragmentary remains of timber buildings with rubbish pits to the rear (centre), and Roman masonry structures still standing at this time (top left).

Lincoln in the Middle Ages

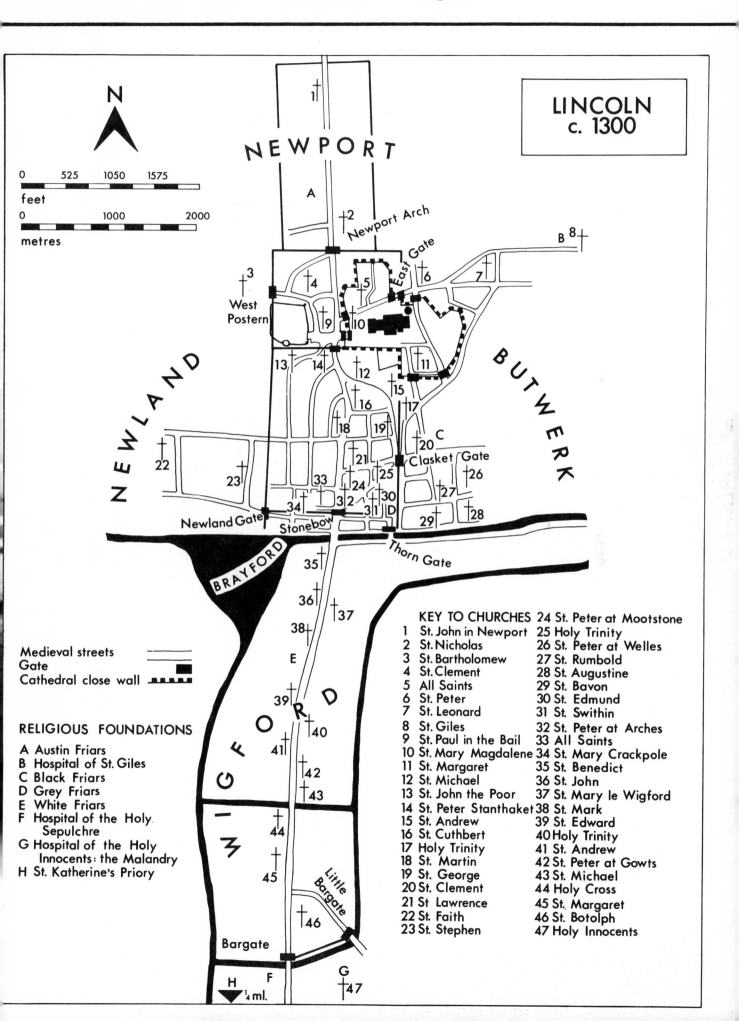

N

0   525   1050   1575
feet

0   1000   2000
metres

NEWPORT

LINCOLN
c. 1300

A

2
Newport Arch

East Gate

B 8

3
West Postern

4

5   6   7

9   10   11

13   14

12

16

15

17

22

18   19

C

20   Clasket Gate

21   25   26

23   33   24   27

34   3 2   30   29   28

31   D

NEWLAND

BUTWERK

Newland Gate
Stonebow

Thorn Gate

BRAYFORD

35

36   37

38

E

39

40

41

42

43

44

45

Little Bargate

46

Bargate

H   F

G   47

Medieval streets
Gate
Cathedral close wall

RELIGIOUS FOUNDATIONS

A Austin Friars
B Hospital of St. Giles
C Black Friars
D Grey Friars
E White Friars
F Hospital of the Holy
    Sepulchre
G Hospital of the Holy
    Innocents: the Malandry
H St. Katherine's Priory

KEY TO CHURCHES	
1 St. John in Newport	24 St. Peter at Mootstone
2 St. Nicholas	25 Holy Trinity
3 St. Bartholomew	26 St. Peter at Welles
4 St. Clement	27 St. Rumbold
5 All Saints	28 St. Augustine
6 St. Peter	29 St. Bavon
7 St. Leonard	30 St. Edmund
8 St. Giles	31 St. Swithin
9 St. Paul in the Bail	32 St. Peter at Arches
10 St. Mary Magdalene	33 All Saints
11 St. Margaret	34 St. Mary Crackpole
12 St. Michael	35 St. Benedict
13 St. John the Poor	36 St. John
14 St. Peter Stanthaket	37 St. Mary le Wigford
15 St. Andrew	38 St. Mark
16 St. Cuthbert	39 St. Edward
17 Holy Trinity	40 Holy Trinity
18 St. Martin	41 St. Andrew
19 St. George	42 St. Peter at Gowts
20 St. Clement	43 St. Michael
21 St. Lawrence	44 Holy Cross
22 St. Faith	45 St. Margaret
23 St. Stephen	46 St. Botolph
	47 Holy Innocents

¼ ml.

The Norman Conquest had a profound effect on the physical layout of the upper city. In 1068 William the Conqueror ordered the construction of the castle, built in the south-western quarter of the upper walled enclosure and incorporating in its bank part of the Roman defences including the Upper West Gate. One consequence was the realignment of the east-west street to the north of the castle, along the line followed by modern Westgate leading to a new postern-gate in the west wall. Another seems to have been the origin of the suburb of Newport beyond the north gate, where it seems likely the inhabitants of the city displaced by the building of the castle were re-settled. The rest of the upper walled enclosure was attached to the castle as the Bail.

The transfer of the see from Dorchester-on-Thames to Lincoln is an example of the Conqueror's policy of establishing cathedrals in major urban centres. Lincoln at this time was probably the third largest town in England, jointly with Norwich, exceeded in terms of population only by London and York: so calculations based on the evidence of the Domesday Survey would suggest. Originally the cathedral of Remigius lay within the walls of the upper town, but as the building was enlarged, part of the east wall of the Bail was demolished to make way for the extensions. The Dean and Chapter gradually acquired substantial property interests in the area, especially to the east outside the Bail. Privacy and protection demanded a new circuit of defences and the crenellated wall of the Cathedral Close with its own towers and gates was built in the late thirteenth and early fourteenth centuries.

Opportunities for large-scale excavations in the upper town are rare, and no archaeological investigation of the medieval remains of this area, apart from current work at St. Paul-in-the-Bail, has been undertaken. Redevelopment schemes have centred on the lower town and recently much information has been gained.

The lower Roman walled town became the medieval city proper, and Wigford, an integral part of the urban scene, remained technically a suburb. The strip of land between the Roman south wall and the river, already an area of commercial importance, became part of the defended enclosure when the walls of the Roman town were extended to the waterside. Details of the extended medieval fortifications on the western side have been forthcoming as a result of archaeological work at Lucy Tower Street on the site now occupied by the new multi-storey car park.

The medieval wall was a substantial structure 7ft. (2.1m.) wide and faced with finely-cut stone. To increase its stability in the marshy ground its foundations included vertical timber piles driven deeply into the mud. Outside the wall lay the huge medieval ditch which in this low-lying part of the town would have been almost filled with water. The full width of the ditch could not be ascertained at Lucy Tower Street but further north at The Park where the medieval ditch represented a remodelling of the late Roman ditch system it was at least 80 ft. (c. 25m.) wide.

The wall terminated at the water's edge with a circular tower whose enigmatic name, the Lucy Tower, has been used since the early seventeenth century, when it is first mentioned in documents, if not before. The tower was still standing in the eighteenth century and an extant drawing shows it crenellated, with narrow slit windows and its chamfered base submerged in reeds. Archaeology pin-pointed its exact location, its date and the details of its construction. The superstructure of the tower, which was hollow, was neatly keyed into the adjoining medieval city wall. Its foundations were similar to those of the wall but of more massive scale with horizontal timbers laid down to give additional support. The tower, the wall and the ditch were contemporary and on the evidence of the pottery, thirteenth century in date. This date is supported by a reference in a late thirteenth-century document to a gate at Newland near the point where the new stretch of fortifications abutted the south-western corner of the Roman circuit.

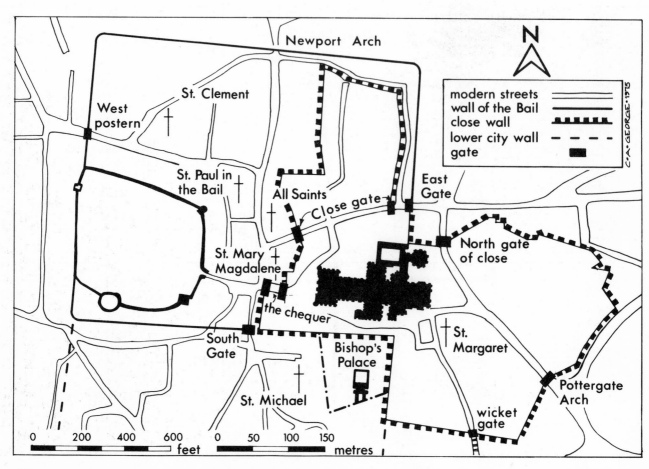

Above: the medieval city wall and the Lucy Tower.
Below: detail of the tower's chamfered plinth and stone and timber foundations.

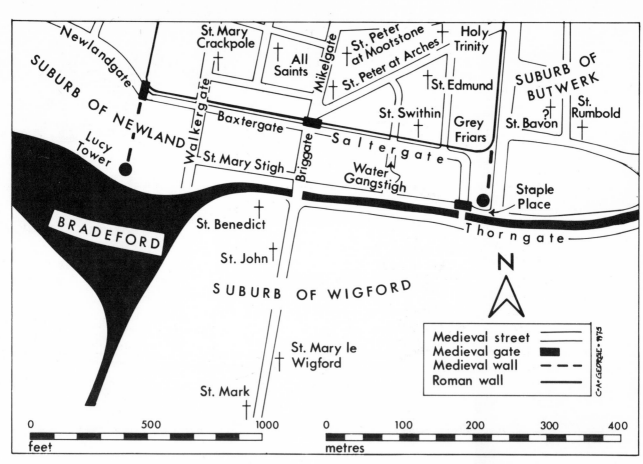

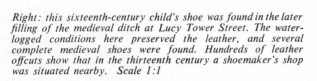

A similar pattern was created on the eastern side of the city. No excavation has yet taken place here to confirm the details of the new defences or to establish their date, but the existence and location of a counterpart to the Lucy Tower near the Green Dragon Inn is indicated by the name Tower Garth on Marrat's map of 1817. The gate on this side, Thorngate, lay not opposite that at Newland but instead controlled access to the bridge across the Witham – an arrangement which reflected the importance of this part of the waterfront.

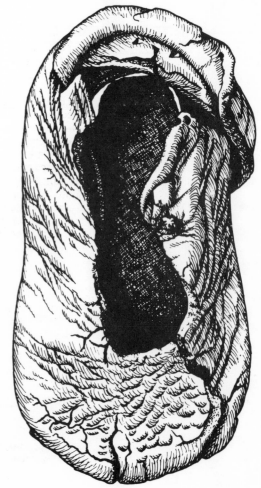

Right: this sixteenth-century child's shoe was found in the later filling of the medieval ditch at Lucy Tower Street. The waterlogged conditions here preserved the leather, and several complete medieval shoes were found. Hundreds of leather offcuts show that in the thirteenth century a shoemaker's shop was situated nearby. Scale 1:1

(Drawn by Marshall Rumbaugh)

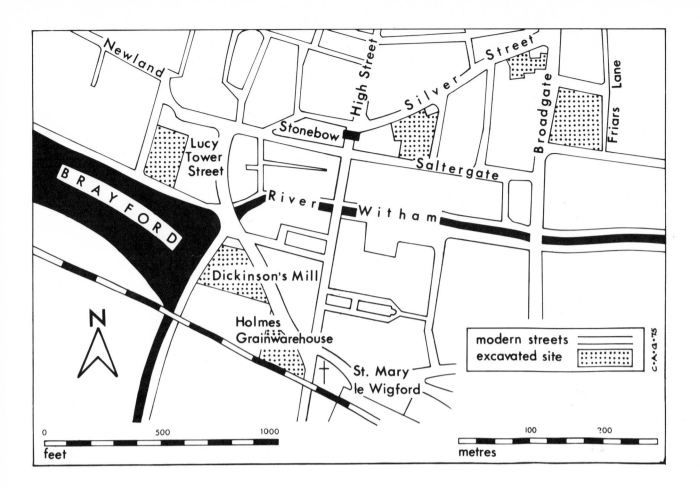

As yet no archaeological work has been undertaken on the waterfront, in spite of its importance in Scandinavian and medieval times, apart from that mentioned above and a small excavation conducted on the eastern bank of the Brayford Pool. Here, on the former site of Dickinson's Mill, between Brayford Wharf East and Wigford Way, the archaeological deposits had been badly damaged by the mill's deep foundations. At the western end of the site, approximately 80 ft. (25m.) to the east of the present waterside, the remains of a timber wharf were uncovered. This consisted of planks bolted together and revetted by vertical timber piles and was probably of thirteenth-century date. Overlying the wharf and projecting in front of it was a stone building constructed on timber pile foundations in the sixteenth century, after the waterfront had been moved further westwards.

Lincoln can boast a large number of standing medieval buildings, many disguised behind more recent facades. The archaeological remains of domestic and commercial properties have recently received attention at the sites of Flaxengate and Danes Terrace near the centre of the medieval city and at Broadgate East in the suburb of Butwerk.

The site at Flaxengate has produced the most detailed information. Not only was there little disturbance to the site from later phases of activity – a rare occurrence in an urban context – but redevelopment of the site has been less pressing, so that time, an all-important factor for successful archaeological work, has been available for the recovery of detailed evidence.

Below: early medieval bone skate found at the site of Holmes Grainwarehouse. It would have been secured to the foot by leather thongs passed through the hole at the front and tied around a peg inserted in the rear.   Scale 3:4

Above: excavation of the thirteenth-century levels at the eastern end of Flaxengate site.
Below: plan of the buildings at the corner of Flaxengate and Grantham Street, in the late thirteenth century. Cross-hatching indicates incorporated earlier structures, and broken lines conjectured masonry.

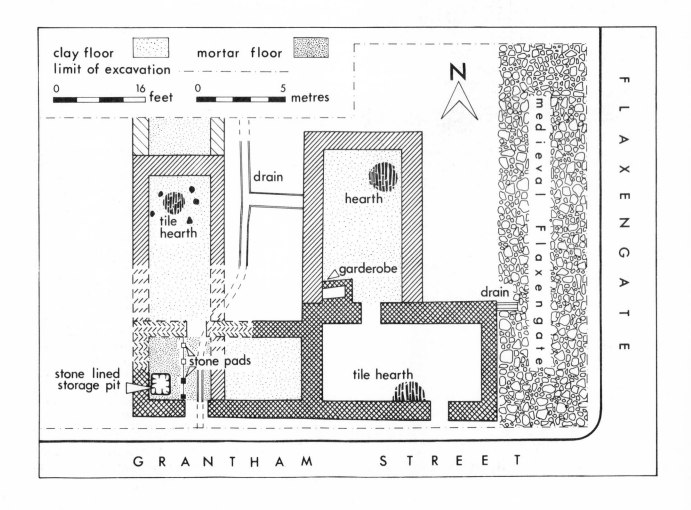

The significance of the site in the Scandinavian period has been discussed. Occupation continued throughout the Norman period with timber buildings along the Grantham Street frontage. The excavation of these was a difficult and complicated process. Fragmentary remains were found, all representing evidence for the walls and internal features of the houses. The positions of the walls were indicated by beam-slots, ground-sills and post-holes, the floors by thin spreads of sand or clay often furnished with clay-based hearths. Also recovered were nails from the timber frame or the roof and pieces of daub, some with wattle impressions, from the walls. Coins of Ethelred II (979–1016), Canute (1016–35), William I (1066–87) and William II (1087–1100), provided useful dating. The street of Flaxengate itself, which in the tenth century had been cobbled, showed little sign of effective resurfacing until the thirteenth century although it appears to have remained a routeway throughout. A boundary fence represented by a row of stakeholes and associated with an eleventh-century building at the corner of Flaxengate and Grantham Street encroached on to the western margin of the roadway.

Flaxengate: above right, stone-lined drain
right, stone-lined garderobe pit
below, street surfaces of medieval Flaxengate.

Timber construction gave way to stone in the late twelfth or early thirteenth centuries. The first stone buildings on the site lay along Grantham Street and followed the same plan as their immediate timber predecessors. The earliest stood at the corner of Flaxengate and Grantham Street. It contained a large hearth in its south-eastern corner, a stone-lined drain led from its eastern wall to the street, and a stone-built garderobe pit was incorporated into its north-western corner. The street of Flaxengate was solidly cobbled soon after the construction of this building and was subsequently resurfaced several times. In the early part of the thirteenth century at least two more buildings were erected fronting on to Grantham Street, then known as Brancegate. They were initially simple structures, strongly built with well-mortared walls, clay floors and stone hearths, and had open yards to the rear containing rubbish pits.

This was a prosperous area in the thirteenth century. The surviving documents attest to the presence in the vicinity of wealthy merchants, some of them Jewish. Later in the thirteenth century two of the buildings were extended at the rear to form large L-shaped structures with small open yards between. The rooms along the street frontage seem to have been used for commercial activities and the spacious new rooms at the rear as domestic accommodation. In one building a narrow internal passageway led from the street directly to the domestic quarters. Malting kilns and loom-weights help illustrate the activities of the inhabitants, and the discovery of a gold ring and gold pin attests to their degree of wealth.

Flaxengate: above right, medieval gold jewellery. Scale 3:1 above left, selection of medieval lead weights. Scale 1:1

Below: medieval belt plate found at Flaxengate, made of bronze inlaid with coloured enamel and depicting a formal beast, half dog, half lion. Like so many metal objects it had corroded badly in the soil. On excavation the object could not be identified and none of the decoration was visible to the naked eye, although it showed clearly on the X-ray plate (left).

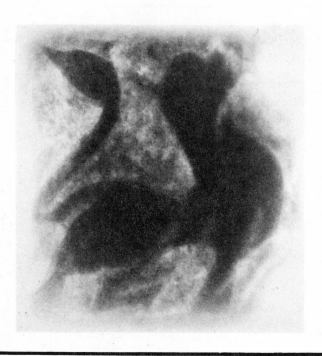

In the fifteenth century most of the thirteenth-century structures were demolished, although some of the walls along the Grantham Street frontage were incorporated into the new buildings. These lay only at the eastern end of the site and were narrow buildings, less substantially constructed than those which had previously stood on the site. One of the fifteenth-century properties may have been a commercial bakery. It was sited at the corner of Flaxengate and Grantham Street and contained a succession of four large ovens each with a sunken floor made of pitched re-used roofing tiles. In the post-medieval period the site was largely derelict until a row of houses was built in the nineteenth century.

Flaxengate: above, fifteenth-century oven, below, malting-kiln.

Part of the Malandry coin hoard. About eight hundred silver coins of Henry I (1100-35), some rare issues, were found during construction work at South Park open-air school. The coins had been buried in a cloth container and were declared Treasure Trove by a coroner's inquest. Also known as the Hospital of the Holy Innocents, the Malandry was a leper hospital founded by the early twelfth century just outside the southern limits of Wigford. (Photograph by courtesy of Lincoln City and County Museum)

Excavations undertaken in 1974 on Steep Hill and on a site at Danes Terrace have shown how the constructional problems posed by the gradient of the hill were faced by the medieval builders. At Steep Hill, on a small site adjacent to Jews' Court, the first medieval stone building, which was Norman in date, had been terraced into the hillside, set down below the level of the remains of demolished Roman buildings.

Two areas containing medieval stone buildings have been investigated at Danes Terrace, one where it adjoins the Strait where the land is still relatively flat, the other at its junction with Flaxengate where the hill begins to rise steeply. Three substantial stone buildings stood gable-ended on to Danes Terrace on this latter site in the thirteenth century, each free-standing with passageways between and heavily terraced into the hillside. The corner property was the first to be erected, probably in the late twelfth century. It had a room at ground-floor level fronting on to Danes Terrace, to the south of which lay a vaulted undercroft entered from the south by stairs which led down from the Flaxengate street. This may represent the basement of a separate property fronting on to Flaxengate. Roman walls served as the bases for the main east-west walls of the undercroft. The front and rear rooms of the neighbouring property along Danes Terrace were also divided by a terrace wall, so that it too had floors at different levels. The third building along Danes Terrace, only part of which has so far been excavated, also had a substantial undercroft.

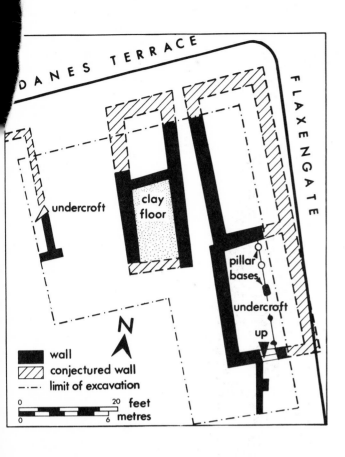

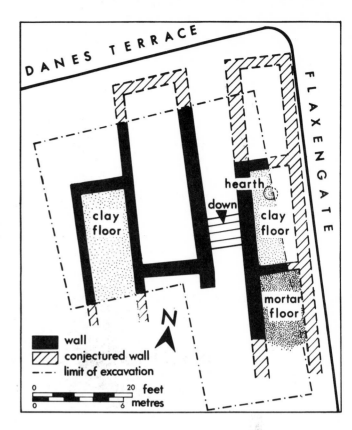

*Danes Terrace: above, medieval stone buildings, period I (left) and period II (right),
below, beads and waste material. Scale 1:1*

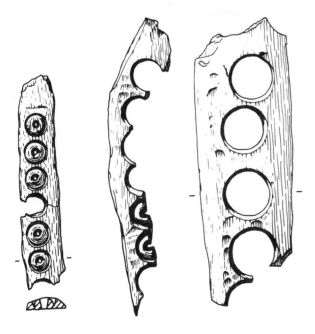

All the buildings here were subsequently remodelled, but the corner property remained free-standing and in the later medieval period the passageway between it and the next property on Danes Terrace was furnished with a flight of steps down to the rear of the buildings. Rebuilding of the other two properties on Danes Terrace dispensed with the former passageway between them. In the fourteenth century activities in the area included the manufacture of beads or buttons produced from animal bone, and large quantities of offcuts and waste material were found.

Terracing was not so marked at the western end of the site where Danes Terrace joins the Strait. Remains of two of the later twelfth century stone buldings have been found here fronting on to the Strait. Only part of the southernmost property has been excavated, but the building which stood on the corner was a large house with a layout similar to that of the Jew's House opposite. The alignment of the boundary wall between them, askew to the medieval street, had been dictated by the survival of a substantial Roman wall which had been incorporated into their structure. Some of the rooms of the medieval houses helped serve as the cellars in later buildings on the site, so that one of the property boundaries here preserved the Roman orientation through to the twentieth century. These buildings were demolished and replaced by new properties in the later fifteenth or early sixteenth century. The walls and foundations of this later period contained many architectural fragments re-used from a building which had been demolished. Some of these were similar to the embellishments of the standing Jew's House and it is reasonable to associate them with the earlier stone buildings on the site.

Above: Norman building on Steep Hill known as The Jew's House. Recent archaeological work has shown that nearby there were many houses like this in the later twelfth century.

Left: many fragments of architectural mouldings have been found at Danes Terrace. This example would have supported the arch over a doorway of a twelfth-century building.

Above: fifteenth-century water jugs and a cooking pot associated with a medieval building at the site of Holmes Grainwarehouse and found in a cess-pit where they had been thrown away.

Right: excavating a thirteenth-century jug from a rubbish pit at Broadgate East.

Some information has been gained from excavation about the medieval suburbs of Newland and Butwerk. Newland Gate led out to the suburb of the same name, the word 'Newland' referring to its origin as land reclaimed for settlement from the marshes. When this occurred is uncertain. It is first mentioned in a document soon after the middle of the twelfth century and there is as yet no positive evidence to support its existence at an earlier date. The methods used in land reclamation were evident at Lucy Tower Street where the ground level had been prepared to support the defensive structures. Here the marshy ground had been consolidated by laying down spreads of twigs, reeds and other vegetable matter to form a fibrous layer of matting.

At Broadgate East a wealth of evidence was obtained about the physical development of the suburb of Butwerk whose origin in the Scandinavian period has already been mentioned. Previous knowledge about the suburb was very limited. Some information about its long-demolished churches, although not their precise location, is contained in documentary sources, and two were thought to have lain in this area. Both had shrunken parishes by the early fifteenth century and had become redundant by the Reformation.

Their dedications to St. Bavon and St. Rumbold, Flemish saints, are a reminder of the city's close commercial ties with the Low Countries from an early period. Excavation established that no church lay in this part of the suburb, although one may have stood slightly to the north at Unity Square if the two human skeletons, whose graves had been dug through the Roman levels at the northern end of the site, represented outliers of the cemetery.

The eastern part of the site is now occupied by a multi-storey car park, but during the medieval period it was extensively settled, with a range of buildings tightly packed along the eastern site boundary, now a little used road known as Friars Lane, which once led to the Dominican friary nearby. Excavation showed that the street was in existence long before the friary, since the eleventh century if not before. Another line of properties clustered along the edge of the city ditch which was levelled late in the Elizabethan period and is covered now by the busy main street of Broadgate. Behind the built-up street frontages lay an open space, utilized for the disposal of domestic rubbish and consequently honeycombed with rubbish pits. From pre-Conquest times to the end of the twelfth century the buildings here as at Flaxengate were of timber construction with earthen floors and clay-based hearths. The timber buildings were replaced in the early thirteenth century by a row of stone structures, probably modest artisans' dwellings. Most of their plans were recoverable along Friars Lane but along Broadgate cellars of more recent date had removed much of the evidence. Like those at Flaxengate they were initially of simple plan, becoming more complex as they acquired extensions and as properties were amalgamated. An impressive stone building stood near the north-eastern corner of the site in the late thirteenth or early fourteenth century incorporating walls of earlier houses on the street frontage and straddling the boundary wall between them. Surprisingly the standard of building construction during the thirteenth and fourteenth centuries on this site compared favourably with that found at Flaxengate, in spite of the indication provided by most of the documentary sources that Butwerk was a settlement of relatively humble people.

The site continued to be occupied well into the fifteenth century but the standards of construction declined considerably; walls were unmortared and had no foundations, and no floors were discernible. Consequently it was not possible to establish the function or recover complete plans of the late medieval buildings which were represented only by discontinuous stretches of wall covered by several feet of the sterile brown soil which marked the final decline of Butwerk.

Broadgate East: right, thirteenth-century buildings along Friars Lane. (Photograph by M. J. Jones)

below, plan of buildings at the corner of Unity Square and Friars Lane in the early fourteenth century.

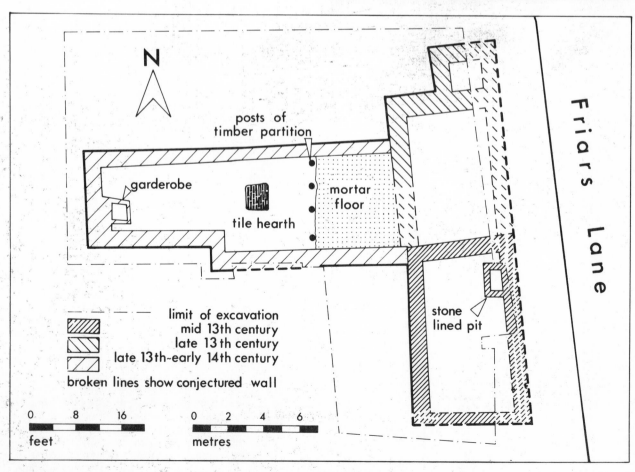

N

posts of timber partition

garderobe

tile hearth

mortar floor

stone lined pit

Friars Lane

limit of excavation
mid 13th century
late 13th century
late 13th-early 14th century
broken lines show conjectured wall

0   8   16
feet

0   2   4   6
metres